PRO FOOTBALL'S

ALL-TIME GREATEST COMEBACKS

BY DREW LYON

CONSULTANT:
BRUCE BERGLUND
PROFESSOR OF HISTORY, CALVIN COLLEGE
GRAND RAPIDS, MICHIGAN

CAPSTONE PRESS
a capstone imprint

Edge Books are published by Capstone Press
1710 Roe Crest Drive, North Mankato, Minnesota 56003
www.mycapstone.com

Library of Congress Cataloging-in-Publication data is available on
the Library of Congress Website.

ISBN 978-1-5435-5434-2 (library binding)
ISBN 978-1-5435-5439-7 (eBook PDF)

Summary: Engaging text and action-packed photos describe the
greatest comeback stories in National Football League history.

EDITORIAL CREDITS
Aaron Sautter, editor; Bob Lentz and Jennifer Bergstrom, designers;
Eric Gohl, media researcher; Tori Abraham, production specialist

PHOTO CREDITS
AP Photo: Todd Rosenberg, cover; Getty Images: David E. Klutho,
28–29, Focus On Sport, 18, John Biever, 9, 17, Kidwiler Collection,
14, Marvin E. Newman, 10–11; Newscom: AI Wire Photo Service/
Rich Kane, 23, Icon Sportswire/Robin Alam, 24, Sipa USA/Anthony
Behar, 20, Sipa USA/Dave Clements, 6, TNS/Curtis Compton, 5, USA
Today Sports/Kyle Terada, 12, USA Today Sports/Troy Taormina, 27;
Shutterstock: Sergey Nivens, 1

Design Elements: Shutterstock

Printed and bound in the United States of America.
PA48

TABLE OF CONTENTS

NEVER SURRENDER

Football is a 60-minute game. Not 30 minutes or even 59 minutes. The New England Patriots made sure football fans remembered that in Super Bowl LI. After falling behind 28–3, the Pats rallied together to achieve the biggest comeback win in Super Bowl history.

The nearly 100-year history of pro football is highlighted by heroic comebacks of all shapes and sizes. Some comebacks take a total team effort. Other comebacks are more personal. Every year some players make inspiring returns from serious injuries or medical conditions.

New England's dramatic 25-point comeback in the 51st Super Bowl tops a long list of National Football League (NFL) comebacks. As many fans know, in pro football no one can be counted out until the game clock strikes zero.

- -

comeback—when a team rallies from behind to win a big game or make it to the playoffs; or when a player overcomes a serious injury or illness to return to the game

Patriots quarterback Tom Brady celebrates winning Super Bowl LI after leading the biggest comeback in Super Bowl history.

CHAPTER 1

NOT OVER 'TIL IT'S OVER

The most dramatic moments in football often come when a team seems to have little hope. But with grit and determination, and a bit of luck, teams can show that gridiron miracles do happen at times.

James White

PATRIOT GAMES

The New England Patriots picked a bad time to play their worst half of the season. The Atlanta Falcons were crushing the Pats 28–3 in the third quarter of Super Bowl LI. Some Patriots fans left Houston's NRG Stadium in disgust. Little did they know what they were about to miss.

Halfway through the third quarter, Tom Brady sparked some hope by leading his team 75 yards to score a touchdown. The Patriots followed that with another TD, a field goal, and a 2-point conversion. The Falcons seemed lost as they watched their lead shrink. With less than a minute left, running back James White snagged yet another TD on a tough run. Brady finished the turnaround with another 2-point conversion. Tie game! The Super Bowl was headed to its first ever overtime game.

New England won the coin flip and got the ball. Brady continued his on-field magic and shredded Atlanta's defense in a 75-yard touchdown drive. Never in playoff history had a team won after trailing by more than 17 points in the fourth quarter. It was the most dramatic victory ever seen in the Super Bowl.

2-point conversion—a score that can be attempted instead of kicking an extra point after a touchdown; the offense is given one play to run or pass the ball from the 2-yard line into the end zone

overtime—an extra period of play if the score is tied at the end of the fourth quarter

drive—a series of plays in which an offense moves into scoring position

PAYBACK
In the NFL, what goes around comes around. In 2018 Brady's Patriots reached the Super Bowl for the 8th time in 17 seasons. But this time, the Philadelphia Eagles came from behind in the fourth quarter and beat the Pats 41–33.

HOUSTON, WE HAVE A PROBLEM

In 1993 the Buffalo Bills achieved an amazing playoff win against the Houston Oilers. The game was so unbelievable that diehard Bills fans simply call it "The Comeback."

The Oilers entered halftime blowing out Buffalo 28–3. Nobody thought the Bills had a chance. The third quarter started even worse for Buffalo. Quarterback Frank Reich threw a pick-six interception, making it 35–3.

But then things began to turn around. Buffalo scored a TD to cut Houston's lead to 35–10. Then the Bills recovered the onside kick. They still had a chance—barely. Then Reich threw three more TD passes to bring his team within four points. The Bills had tallied 28 points in less than seven minutes!

Bills receiver Andre Reed then caught his third score of the game, putting Buffalo ahead 38–35. A late Houston field goal forced overtime, but the tide had turned. Buffalo kicker Steve Christie's overtime field goal completed an NFL-record 32-point comeback victory.

-----

pick-six—a touchdown scored by the defense after intercepting a pass and running the ball to the end zone

interception—a pass caught by a defensive player

onside kick—a short kickoff that can be recovered by the kicking team; the ball must first travel at least 10 yards

Frank Reich

Steve Christie

TO BE FRANK

Frank Reich was a veteran of record-setting comebacks. In college he was the backup quarterback at the University of Maryland. In the 1984 Orange Bowl, Reich led a then–NCAA record 31-point comeback win against the University of Miami. In 2018 Reich was named head coach of the Indianapolis Colts.

A ROARING RECOVERY

The Detroit Lions haven't had much playoff success since the 1950s. But the team's championship run in 1957 was one for the history books.

In the semifinal game against the San Francisco 49ers, Detroit trailed 24–7 at halftime. It seemed all but over for the Lions. An announcement even let 49ers fans know that they could already get tickets for the NFL Championship Game.

But there were still 30 minutes left to go. And the Lions weren't about to go down without a fight. Down 27–7 in the third quarter, Detroit's offense rattled off 24 points. The 49ers couldn't respond with a score of their own. When the dust settled, the Lions upset the 49ers 31–27. At the NFL Championship Game, Detroit routed the Cleveland Browns 59–14 to claim the title.

Steve Junker

Detroit Lions receiver Steve Junker led his team with 109 yards receiving and two touchdowns in the 1957 NFL Championship Game.

Seattle Seahawks wide receiver Jermaine Kearse battled Green Bay Packers cornerback Tramon Williams to score the game-winning touchdown in the 2014 NFC Championship Game.

Tramon Williams

Jermaine Kearse

A SEATTLE STUNNER

Things weren't clicking for the Seattle Seahawks in the 2014 NFC Championship Game against the Green Bay Packers. At halftime they trailed the Packers 16–0. Seattle finally got on the board with a TD late in the third quarter. But the Packers put up a field goal to extend their lead to 19–7.

Then things turned around late in the fourth quarter. With just over two minutes left, Seahawks quarterback Russell Wilson ran in a touchdown. Seattle managed to recover the onside kick, and four plays later scored another TD. The 'Hawks had taken a 3-point lead, but it wasn't over yet. Packers quarterback Aaron Rodgers led a desperate drive to score a field goal to force overtime.

During overtime, Wilson took just six plays to hit Jermaine Kearse for the game-winning touchdown. In the span of a few minutes, Seattle had pulled off the biggest comeback in NFC Championship Game history.

COLTS PAYBACK
In the 2006 AFC Championship Game, the New England Patriots were headed toward another win over the Indianapolis Colts. But quarterback Peyton Manning closed a 15-point gap to defeat Tom Brady's Patriots. The comeback was a Conference Championship game record that stood until Seattle's win over Green Bay.

CHAPTER 2

THE COMEBACK CAPTAINS

To be successful a team needs a great captain to lead the charge. This is especially true when a team falls behind. When there seems to be little hope, a great quarterback can still inspire and lead his team to victory.

Johnny Unitas

THE GREATEST GAME EVER PLAYED

In the 1950s pro football wasn't exactly must-see TV. But the 1958 NFL Championship Game between the Baltimore Colts and the New York Giants was a game changer.

The Colts led 14–3 at halftime before New York scored 14 straight points to retake the lead. At home 45 million people watched their black-and-white TV sets as Colts quarterback Johnny Unitas became an instant star. He hurried his team down the field in the first ever two-minute drill.

Unitas led the Colts to score a field goal and force the first sudden-death game in NFL playoff history. Calling his own plays in overtime, "Johnny U" marched his team 80 yards down the field to score the game winner. It was a thrilling end to what football historians now call The Greatest Game Ever Played.

two-minute drill—a series of plays run by an offense to try to score quickly, usually when there are two minutes or less left on the game clock

MUST-SEE TV
The 1958 title game was broadcast across America, sparking the NFL's popularity. In 2008 NFL Films produced a two-hour movie that restored the footage of the game in full color.

"THE DRIVE"

Quarterback John Elway had a tough task ahead of him. His Denver Broncos team was facing the Cleveland Browns in the 1986 AFC Championship Game. The Broncos were down by a touchdown with just five minutes left. As the Denver offense gathered at its own 2-yard line, the team faced a long 98 yards to hit pay dirt.

But Elway wasn't scared. The Denver gunslinger excelled during clutch moments. In a 15-play masterpiece, Elway used his arm and his legs to move Denver within striking range. Cleveland's fans watched helplessly as Elway inched closer to the tying touchdown.

With just 39 seconds left, Elway found Mark Jackson for a 5-yard score. Then Rich Karlis kicked the extra point to tie the game. Denver went on to win in overtime, and Elway became a comeback legend.

THE DRIVE, PART 2

In the 1991 AFC Divisional Playoffs, Elway was again called upon to save the Broncos' season. Down 24–23 against Houston, Elway repeated his 1986 heroics. He showed off his skills with a combination of scrambling runs and throws. Denver kicked a field goal to win in the final seconds, growing Elway's status as a football legend.

John Elway

During his career John Elway led the Denver Broncos to five Super Bowls and two titles in 1998 and 1999.

Joe Montana

"THE CATCH"

Montana became a household name during the 1981 season. In the final minutes of the NFC Championship Game, he led the 49ers on an 89-yard, game-winning drive. Montana's fade away end zone completion to receiver Dwight Clark was given the nickname "The Catch."

KEEPING HIS COOL

Hall of Fame quarterback Joe Montana's nickname was "Joe Cool." And he earned it for good reason. He was always calm under pressure.

In 1989 Montana's cool head served him well during the final minutes of Super Bowl XXIII in Miami. His San Francisco 49ers trailed the Cincinnati Bengals 16–13 with a little more than three minutes to go. Montana gathered his team in the huddle, 92 yards away from the end zone.

The pressure was on, but Joe Cool wasn't feeling the heat. The two-minute drill was one of his specialties. Montana kept the mood light in the huddle. Looking toward the crowd, he pointed out a famous actor who was watching from the stands. Montana's message to his team was clear: Relax, fellas. It's just a game.

Montana picked apart Cincinnati's defense. On the 11th play of the drive, Montana tossed a touchdown strike to receiver John Taylor. Montana had barely broken a sweat. For Joe Cool, it was all in a day's work.

----

end zone—the area between the goal line and the end line at either end of a football field

CHAPTER 3

GRIDIRON GRIT

Coming from behind to win a big game can be thrilling. But some great comebacks are more personal. Sometimes players face impossible odds to find success or come back from a serious injury or illness. With hard work and determination, great players find ways to overcome the odds.

Peyton Manning

PEYTON'S PAYBACK

Nobody thought Indianapolis Colts quarterback Peyton Manning would ever wear a different jersey. But in 2011 a neck injury threatened to end his amazing career. Some experts feared a hard hit on the star QB could even affect his ability to walk.

Manning chose to have spinal fusion surgery and sat out the 2011 season. Then amazingly, the Colts let Manning go. But he wasn't ready to retire just yet. After more than a decade of greatness in Indy, he signed with the Denver Broncos.

Manning proved he still had juice in his throwing arm. In 2012 he led Denver to a 13–3 record and won the Comeback Player of the Year award. But he wasn't done yet. In 2013 "The Sheriff" shattered the NFL record for touchdown passes in a season (55). He was also named the NFL's Most Valuable Player (MVP) that year. In the final game of Manning's incredible career, he helped the Broncos win Super Bowl 50. He retired as the NFL's greatest statistical quarterback and the all-time leader in fourth quarter comebacks.

ELITE ELI

Peyton's younger brother, Eli, is also no stranger to legendary comebacks. Eli twice led the New York Giants to thrilling last-minute comebacks against the New England Patriots in Super Bowls XLII and XLVI. In both games, Peyton Manning watched and cheered on his younger brother from the stands. Their father, Archie, was also a quarterback in the NFL for 13 years.

THE BIG SHORT

At every level of football, critics believed that Doug Flutie was too short to be a quarterback. He proved them all wrong.

Standing at 5 feet, 9 inches (175 centimeters) tall, Flutie first burst onto the scene at Boston College. During his senior year, he completed an epic bomb pass, called a "Hail Flutie," to hand the Miami Hurricanes a stunning last-second defeat. However, pro scouts still thought that Flutie was too small to make it in the NFL.

Flutie did play in the NFL for a few years but didn't find much success. However, everything changed in 1990. Flutie found his calling playing in the Canadian Football League (CFL). From 1990 to 1997 he led the CFL in passing for five seasons and won three championships. He was also named the CFL's Most Outstanding Player a record six times.

But Flutie had unfinished business in the NFL. In 1998 he signed with the Buffalo Bills. The mobile quarterback fooled defenders with his shifty moves, and he was named Comeback Player of the Year. Flutie went on to play another seven years in the NFL before hanging up his helmet for the last time. Time and time again, Doug Flutie showed that small quarterbacks can still play big.

Doug Flutie

YARD STICKS

During the 1991 season with the British Columbia Lions, Flutie threw for 6,619 yards. It remains a professional football record.

Thomas Davis Sr.

A MAN'S MAN

Thomas Davis Sr. is an All-Pro both on and off the field. Davis and his wife, Kelly, started the Thomas Davis Defending Dreams Foundation. The organization provides resources and programs for disadvantaged youth. In 2014 Davis won the NFL's Walter Payton Man of the Year award.

PANTHER PRIDE

Many NFL players struggle to return after the first tear of their anterior cruciate ligament (ACL). However, no player had ever returned from three ACL tears. That is, until Carolina Panthers linebacker Thomas Davis Sr. did it. Each time he was injured, he worked his way back to the gridiron and returned stronger than ever.

"I've never been a quitter at anything I've done in my life," Davis said. "I told myself I was going to make this thing work and make it happen."

Davis not only made it happen, he made it to the Pro Bowl three straight seasons. In 2016 he broke his forearm during the NFC Championship Game. It was no big deal for him. Two weeks later, Davis was suiting up to play in Super Bowl 50. After 14 years with the Panthers, Davis decided that 2018 would be his final season in the NFL.

Pro Bowl—a game played at the end of the NFL season featuring all-star players from both the American Football Conference (AFC) and the National Football Conference (NFC)

SAFETY PLAY

In 2014 Kansas City Chiefs safety Eric Berry was one of the league's top defensive players. Partway through the season, Berry was told he faced an opponent that wouldn't be easy to tackle. He was diagnosed with a type of cancer called Hodgkin's Lymphoma.

"Oh man, it was terrifying at first," Berry recalled. "Just hearing 'You have cancer' — it was tough."

The treatments for his disease ended his season, but Berry vowed to come back. He didn't miss a step. In 2015 Berry earned Comeback Player of the Year honors and was selected for his fourth Pro Bowl appearance. In 2016 Berry signed a new contract with Kansas City that made him the highest paid safety in the NFL.

STEEL RESERVE

In 2015 University of Pittsburgh running back James Conner was also diagnosed with Hodgkin's Lymphoma. He kept practicing with his team while undergoing his cancer treatments. In 2017 Conner was cancer-free and was drafted by his hometown Pittsburgh Steelers. While fighting his cancer, he started a friendship with one of his heroes, Eric Berry.

Eric Berry

OVERTIME:
MORE AMAZING COMEBACKS

"ALL DAY" AP: The one thing NFL players never want to hear is "torn ACL." Minnesota Vikings running back Adrian Peterson was given that grim diagnosis in December 2011. He'd also torn a second ligament in his left knee. But Peterson was determined to return to the gridiron in time for the next season, and he did. In 2012 Peterson came back and ran for 2,097 yards, the second most in a season in NFL history. He was also named the NFL's MVP that year.

- -

THE MUSIC CITY MIRACLE: In the 1999 AFC Wild Card Game the Buffalo Bills took a one-point lead with just 16 seconds left. The Tennessee Titans had almost no hope. But when the Titans' Lorenzo Neal received the final kickoff, he handed the ball off to Frank Wycheck. Wycheck then turned and threw a lateral pass to Kevin Dyson near the sideline. The play caught the Bills by surprise. Not a single defender stood in Dyson's path. He galloped 75 yards to the end zone in one of the NFL's most unbelievable come-from-behind wins.

- -

0-4 CHARGERS: In the modern NFL, teams that start the season 0–2 have about a 12 percent chance of making the playoffs. When a team starts 0–4, their chances of making the playoffs drop to about 1 percent. The 1992 San Diego Chargers were the exception to the rule. They started the season 0–4, then won 11 of their final 12 games. They became the only 0–4 team to later reach the playoffs.

THE MINNEAPOLIS MIRACLE: The New Orleans Saints led 24–23 over the Minnesota Vikings in the 2018 NFC Divisional Playoff. Faithful Vikings fans prepared for yet another heartbreaking playoff loss. With just 10 seconds left on the clock, Vikings quarterback Case Keenum took the shotgun snap and heaved the ball to receiver Stefon Diggs at the Saints 34-yard line. Nobody expected what came next. As Diggs leaped to catch the pass, a Saints defender tumbled past him. Diggs landed with the ball and found an empty field in front of him. He raced to the end zone for the last-second game-winning score.

Stefon Diggs

GLOSSARY

2-point conversion (TWO-POYNT kuhn-VER-szhun)—a score that can be attempted instead of kicking an extra point after a touchdown; the offense is given one play to run or pass the ball from the 2-yard line into the end zone

comeback (KUHM-back)—when a team rallies from behind to win a big game or make it to the playoffs; or when a player overcomes a serious injury or illness to return to the game

drive (DRYV)—a series of plays in which an offense moves into scoring position

end zone (END ZOHN)—the area between the goal line and the end line at either end of a football field

interception (in-tur-SEP-shun)—a pass caught by a defensive player

onside kick (ON-side KIK)—a short kickoff that can be recovered by the kicking team; the ball must first travel at least 10 yards

overtime (OH-vur-time)—an extra period of play if the score is tied at the end of the fourth quarter

pick-six (PIK SIX)—a touchdown scored by the defense after intercepting a pass and running the ball to the end zone

Pro Bowl (PRO BOHL)—a game played at the end of the NFL season featuring all-star players from both the American Football Conference (AFC) and the National Football Conference (NFC)

two-minute drill (TOO MIN-uht DRIL)—a series of plays run by an offense to try to score quickly, usually when there are two minutes or less left on the game clock

READ MORE

Bradley, Michael. *Pro Football's Underdogs: Players and Teams Who Shocked the Football World.* Sports Shockers. North Mankato, Minn.: Capstone Press, 2018.

Braun, Eric. *Super Bowl Surprises.* Everything Super Bowl. North Mankato, Minn.: Capstone Press, 2017.

Hall, Brian. *NFL's Top 10 Comebacks.* NFL's Top Ten. Minneapolis: ABDO Publishing, 2017.

INTERNET SITES

Use FactHound to find Internet sites related to this book.

1. Visit *www.facthound.com*

2. Just type in 9781543554342 and go.

Check out projects, games and lots more at
www.capstonekids.com

INDEX